THE

UNION THEOLOGICAL SEMINARY,

IN THE

CITY OF NEW-YORK,

ITS

HISTORY, CONDITION AND WANTS:

AN APPEAL

TO THE

Friends of the Institution.

Published by Order of the Board of Directors.

NEW-YORK:
JOHN F. TROW, PRINTER, 49 ANN-STREET.
1852.

UNION THEOLOGICAL SEMINARY.

This Seminary, situated in the city of New-York, has now been in existence for sixteen years. Its Directors are convinced that the time has come to present to the Christian public a full statement of its condition and prospects, with a view of immediately placing it upon a secure basis.

The following account of its origin and of the designs of its founders was published by themselves:—

"A number of Christians, both clergymen and laymen, in the cities of New-York and Brooklyn, deeply impressed with the claims of the world upon the Church of Christ, to furnish a competent supply of well-educated and pious ministers of the Gospel; impressed also with the inadequacy of all existing means for this purpose; and believing that large cities furnish many peculiar facilities and advantages for conducting theological education; having, after several meetings for consultation and prayer, again convened on the 18th January, A. D. 1836, unanimously adopted the following resolution and declarations:—

"1. RESOLVED, in humble dependence on the grace of God, to attempt the establishment of a Theological Seminary in the city of New-York.

"2. In this Institution, it is the design of the founders to furnish the means of a full and thorough education, in all the subjects taught in the best Theological Seminaries in this or other countries.

"3. Being fully persuaded that vital godliness, a thorough education, and practical training in the works of benevolence and pastoral labor, are all essential to meet the wants and promote the best interests of the kingdom of Christ, the founders of this Seminary design that its students, remaining under pastoral influence, and performing the duties of church-members in the several churches to which they belong, or with which they worship, in prayer-meetings, in the instruction of Sabbath schools and Bible classes, and being conversant with all the benevolent efforts of the present day in this great community, shall have the opportunity of adding to solid learning and true piety, the teachings of experience.

"4. By the foregoing advantages, the founders hope and expect, with the blessing of God, to call forth and enlist in the service of Christ and in the work of the ministry, genius, talent, enlightened piety, and missionary zeal; and to qualify many for the labors and management of the various religious institutions, seminaries of learning, and enterprises of benevolence, which characterize the present times.

"5. In short, it is the design of the founders, to provide a Theological Seminary in the midst of the greatest and most growing community in the United States, which may commend itself to all men of moderate views and feelings, who desire to live free from party strife, and to stand aloof from all extremes of doctrine or of practice."

To accomplish this object, subscriptions were obtained to the amount of about $80,000. This was thought sufficient to sustain the Institution for five years, after which, if it should prove itself worthy of support, it was intended to procure other subscriptions to place the Seminary on a permanent foundation.

The following extracts from the Constitution of the Seminary will show its general character:—

Directors.

"No person shall be eligible to the office of Director, unless he be a minister or member in good standing of some evangelical church, receiving the Westminster Confession of Faith as adopted by the Presbyterian churches in this country.

"Every Director, on entering upon his office, and

also after each re-election, shall make the following declaration, in the presence of the Board, viz.:—

"Approving of the plan and Constitution of the Union Theological Seminary in the city of New-York, and of the Westminster Confession of Faith, and the Presbyterian Form of Church Government, I do solemnly promise to maintain the same, so long as I shall continue to be a member of the Board of Directors."

The Faculty.

"The Faculty shall consist of the Professors of the Seminary, who shall be ordained ministers of the Gospel; one of whom may, by the appointment of the Board, sustain the office of President.

"Every member of the Faculty shall, on entering upon his office, and at the end of every four years thereafter, so long as he remains in office, make and subscribe the following declaration in the presence of the Board, viz.:—

"I believe the Scriptures of the Old and New Testament to be the Word of God, the only infallible rule of faith and practice; and I do now, in the presence of God and the Directors of this Seminary, solemnly and sincerely receive and adopt the Westminster Confession of Faith, as containing the system of doctrine taught in the Holy Scriptures. I do also, in like manner, approve of the Presbyterian Form of Government; and I do solemnly promise that I will not teach or inculcate any thing which shall appear to me to be subversive of the said system of doctrine, or of the principles of said Form of Government, so long as I shall continue to be a Professor in this Seminary."

Students.

"This Seminary shall be open for the admission of students of the requisite qualifications from every denomination of Christians."

"In ordinary cases, no student shall be admitted into the Seminary unless he furnish to the Faculty satisfactory evidence that he has had a regular college education, and testimonials of moral character, of piety, and of his good standing in some evangelical church."

The Progress of the Seminary.

The Institution was opened for instruction December 5, 1836; it was incorporated by the Legislature of the State of New-York, March 17, 1839. Scarcely had it commenced its operations, when financial reverses occurred which made it impossible for several of the subscribers to meet their engagements. The pecuniary embarrassments of 1837 and the following years were felt by us in common with the other benevolent institutions. The difficulties have at times been so formidable, that had it not been for great exertions and patience on the part of its founders and professors, it must have been discontinued. To the very liberal aid of a few friends it is indebted, under God, that it did not perish in these times of severe visitation. Tried thus by adversity almost from the beginning of its existence, it has still, through the Divine favor, held on its way; and it has been instrumental of such good results that its trials, severe as they have been, are not worthy to be mentioned in the comparison.

It has sent forth 314 ministers of the Gospel in the fourteen classes which have already been graduated, being an average of more than 22 for each year. Of these, the number now living is 297, who are engaged in their work, some in neighboring churches, others in the distant portions of our own land, and others in foreign countries. With peculiar praise to God, would its founders recognize the fact that this Seminary has been to so large an extent a Missionary school. Missionaries, and the friends of missions, offer many thanksgivings in its behalf. A well-known and beloved missionary from Constantinople,* has recently borne unequivocal tes-

* Dr. Perkins also writes under date, Oroomiah, June 24th, as follows, to Dr. Robinson:

"Our mission naturally feel a deep interest in yourself personally, as well as in your labors—half its members having been

timony to the special fitness of our students for the work of Foreign Missions. It has equal reputation in the character of the pastors it has supplied to our churches at home, and in the zeal and success of the Home Missionaries it has sent forth. Of the members of the last class, one is to labor in India, another in Syria, a third in Panama, a fourth in San Francisco. For such results the founders and directors of the Seminary feel themselves to be under high and special obligations to the grace and providence of God.

The Institution, in respect both to its management and the character of the instruction given in it, has not departed from the plan of its founders. For sixteen years it has commended itself to "all men of moderate views and feelings, who desire to live free from party strife, and to stand aloof from all extremes of doctrine or of practice." That it has been able to do so during the years in which various forms of fanatical excitement and excess have been so unusually predominant, has secured for it in no small measure the entire confidence of discreet and thoughtful men. Of this the founders have

your pupils. Yours is a privileged work. How numerously is your Seminary now represented on missionary ground! How nobly does it rival all its elder sisters, in furnishing men for the foreign field! I could not desire for it a richer blessing, than that its officers and members may enjoy an unceasing unction of the missionary spirit."

the most gratifying evidence. And it has truly been a Union Seminary. It has not been noted in the field of partisan controversy, nor has it been suspected of unfaithfulness to the truth. In its whole history, and in its present character, it answers to the purpose for which it was established. It has contributed, so far as has been in its power, to the promotion of union among Christians, and to the allaying of sectarian and sectional strife. It has received generous aid from men connected with different branches of Christ's church. Standing upon the general basis of the Westminster Confession of Faith, there is nothing in its position or history which alienates it from any who stand on this basis. The tone of its instructions has always been in harmony with the evangelical theology of our whole country.

The education which this Seminary has given has not been confined to men of a single locality or section of our country. It has educated men from all parts of our land, and for all parts of our land. It has educated, too, men of different denominations. In this respect, also, it deserves its name and answers its intent. The Alumni of this Seminary are from 32 colleges all over our country. Of the graduates of New England colleges it has educated 135; of the New-York City University, 50; of Union College, 30; and in like proportion for the colleges in the Middle, Southern, and Southwestern

States. Of our graduates 90 have been from the New England States; from New-York State and city, 154; from the States west and south of New York, 66; from foreign countries, 5. Of the students now in the Seminary, 29 are from New-York State and city, 15 from New England, 28 from States west and south of New-York, and one from Ireland. Presbyterians, Congregationalists, Baptists, and Methodists, have all participated in the advantages of the Seminary to their common benefit. In the light of such facts, we see the importance of the central position of the Seminary, and the value of its special characteristics as a Union Theological Institution.

And in the number of its students, it has been signally favored. In spite of all the disadvantages under which it has labored, in the number of its graduates it has been one of the first three Theological Seminaries of our land. Several years it has stood the second. Had it possessed the full endowments, and offered all the privileges and attractions of our older institutions, we believe that in point of numbers it would have been second to none. As it is, its growth and prosperity in respect to the number of its students have been unequalled by any similar institution.

The professorships of the Seminary have been filled by those who have commanded the confidence of the Christian community. Besides the instruction given by professors extraordinary in various branches, Rev. Dr. White was the professor of Systematic Theology from the origin of the institution to his lamented decease in August, 1850. Dr. Robinson has been professor of Biblical Literature since 1837. The Rev. T. H. Skinner, D. D., took the chair of Sacred Rhetoric and Pastoral Theology in 1848. At the time that the death of Dr. White had made a vacancy in the faculty, the Board were notified of the acceptance of the chair of Church History by Professor Henry B. Smith. This department had been previously filled, in part, by the lectures of Dr. Halsey for two successive years, but chiefly by the generous services of Rev. Dr. S. H. Cox. During the last year, the vacancy left by the decease of Rev. Dr. White has been supplied by the accession of Rev. Jas. P. Wilson, D. D., of Philadelphia, to the department of Systematic Theology. From 1842, William W. Turner, A. M., has been a constant and thorough instructor in the elements of the Hebrew language. And now all the departments of instruction in the Seminary are filled, and in successful operation. And contemporaneously with this, the favorable decision of a lawsuit has put the Institution in possession of a very valuable legacy from James Roosevelt, Esq., lately deceased. The general condition of the Seminary in respect to instruction, and students, and the confidence of the community, has never been more satisfactory and encouraging than it is at present.

The Location of the Seminary in the City of New-York.

When this Seminary was projected, it was extensively doubted whether its location in a large commercial metropolis would be favorable to the objects of a theological institution. The conviction of the founders that it was so, rested on general views, which, in this country, had not been tested by experience. Time has confirmed that conviction. During the whole period of its existence the Seminary has been growing stronger and stronger; and it has been becoming increasingly evident, that the reasons for establishing schools of law and medicine in large cities, rather than in more secluded situations, are equally strong in favor of such a preference as to the location of a theological school.

It has been extensively supposed that secluded retreats, far from the excitements of active life, and the tumult and worldliness of great cities, were the only fitting places to prepare our young men for the ministry of the Gospel. So strong has been this conviction, that it has, at least in part, determined the location of our chief schools of theology. The experience of the Union Theological Seminary has brought out the advantages of a large city in striking contrast with the prejudices against it. Many who at first regarded it with doubt and distrust, are now convinced. Seclusion is not what a student of theology, a future minister for our age and country, most needs. He requires thorough discipline, he needs meditation, but he also needs to be prepared for the discharge of the special duties of his profession. If he has always lived in retirement, his ideas of life will inevitably be wrong. After completing his education, called at once, as he will probably be, to the active duties of the ministry, he has still to learn how as a man to move among men—he has still to unlearn his too scholastic habits. He finds his true position with difficulty. He has the theory, and but little of the practice of his profession. In a great city the theory and the practice of the profession are more likely to be acquired together.

It has been thought that the distractions of a city are unfavorable to the highest mental discipline and culture. The experience of the old world certainly refutes this objection. All the great schools of Europe, the sources of the highest discipline and cultivation, are in large places. And it is confidently believed that the students of our Seminary will compare favorably with those of any similar institution, in their acquisitions and mental discipline, as well as in the facility of using their knowledge. Our theological students are generally mature in mind and character; and this saves them from many of the perils incident to young men in a large city, and enables them to enjoy its advantages without being injured by its disadvantages.

And the advantages are many. Thought and feeling are both stimulated. Formal, and, it may be, rustic habits are worn away. Human life is seen in many of its phases. Ignorance, and vice, and moral evil, in all their forms, touch the heart and lead to effort. In visiting, while in the Seminary, the poor, the destitute and the abandoned, in ministering to the spiritual wants of prisoners and outcasts, in gathering Sabbath schools among the neglected and unruly, our students are trained for their work, for a work which is needed all over the world. They come to understand the wants of that class of society which most needs to be reached by the Gospel. And this they can do, as they have done, not only without detriment to their studies, but rather getting the right tone and spirit for the real study of the truth as it is in Jesus. In contact also with the great benevolent institutions which have their centre here, they catch more of their spirit, and the officers of these institutions are able, from personal knowledge, to select wisely the men who are fitted for their service. Much is done by the students in connection with the Tract and Bible

Societies, the City Missions and Sabbath Schools. And no one can estimate the salutary influence thus exerted by a hundred pious young men, in their connection and intercourse with the churches and the community. Here, too, where all the influences that threaten danger to our moral and religious interests as a people do most congregate, and are most distinctly proclaimed, our young men may learn the true nature and real hazard of these tendencies as they could not in more secluded spheres. The ministers of the next generation are to fight a hard contest with manifold forms of error and of unbelief; it is well for them, then, to be trained where the elements of the contest are most decisively felt, and can be most practically studied. The work of the ministry is so diversified, that the very diversities of a city life offer peculiar advantages in the education of ministers. And here, too, are found the best and most varied models of professional ability, in full and earnest activity. The student may observe, and compare, and appropriate. He will not receive the exclusive impress of one predominant mind, and this is favorable to his own individuality. He hears those who are among the most eminent, as preachers, as lecturers, as orators; he hears all the great topics of the day discussed by those who have mastered them; his mind is stimulated to a healthful activity. The refining influences of a cultivated and various social life have also a favorable effect upon the general character and deportment of young men, giving them facility and ease in the intercourse of society.

The history of the Seminary has also given abundant proof of the excellence of its location, in affording facilities for indigent students to support themselves while prosecuting their studies. Most young men who enter our seminaries are poor—some are very poor. In teaching, or in other laudable avocations, probably more than half of our students find an adequate maintenance. Any young man with special qualifications or gifts, can be more sure of finding employment for them in a large city than in a more quiet community.

The advantage of establishing a Theological Seminary in the heart of the city of New-York cannot be considered any longer as a mere experiment. It is no longer a matter of doubt whether the advantages are not much greater than the disadvantages. It has been abundantly proved that young men will come to such an institution if they can secure their support, and a thorough education. It has been proved that they are there qualified for the best and highest usefulness. The Institution, as to its location, has more than answered the expectations with which it was established. In view of the character and prospective greatness of the city of

New-York, of the influence which it must needs have upon the American people, of its relations to all the great religious and moral interests of the whole country; and in view, also, of what the experience of our Institution has taught us, it is scarcely to be doubted that a more desirable location for a Theological Seminary of the highest order is not to be found than which is now occupied by the Union Theological Seminary.

What a Theological Seminary in New-York ought to be.

Much as has already been accomplished by this Seminary, the Directors are convinced that only a beginning has been made, that the Institution has thus far been only growing towards the character and shape which it ought to assume. The times and the wants of our country, and of the world, demand that we should here have a Theological School of the very highest character. If the Union Seminary is to accomplish the work to which Providence seems to have called it, it must be reinvigorated, and supported with a still larger charity. There ought to be in the city of New-York an evangelical school of theology of such a character, so well appointed, and offering such facilities and accommodations to students, that the young men of our churches from all parts of the land might be invited to come to it, with the assurance that they should have all the facilities needed for the attainment of the most thorough theological education. To make full proof of the advantanges of such a central and influential location, the Institution must be organized and endowed on a comprehensive plan. Situated in an expensive city, it requires for its ordinary administration larger funds than would be needed in more quiet retreats. The advantages of the location are to be the compensation for the increased expenditures. If the location have the advantages which we have described, Christian wisdom demands that the means be supplied for realizing all these advantages in their fullest measure; if young men can here be best trained for the diversified work of the Christian ministry, the means for such training ought to be supplied with a liberal hand.

Even in the best and oldest of our seminaries, the means and facilities for the most thorough training in the science of theology are only too restricted; and the need of cultivating theology, and of training our young men to thorough theological investigations, is increasing from year to year. As sects increase, as Romanism advances, as infidelity in various forms lifts up its voice, the churches are bound to educate her teachers, so that they shall be fitted for the work to which they are thereby called. We ought to have here an Institution which shall offer unusual facilities to any who may be willing to devote themselves, specially and earnestly, to any great branch of theological investigation. Many of our young men who intend to devote themselves to a more scholastic vocation than the usual work of the ministry, now feel that there is no place where they can pursue their studies with the necessary facilities and aids. They usually go to the seminaries and universities of foreign lands. Some of the most promising young men of every graduating class ought to be delayed from entering upon the immediate preaching of the Gospel, and pursue an additional course of study. Had we the means, could we give them but a support for two or three years, in ten or twenty years the whole Church would feel the benefit. And by directing the studies of such young men, the professors of the Seminary would be constantly stimulated to thorough investigations beyond the ordinary routine of instruction. A Seminary in the city of New-York ought to have the training of such young men in special courses of study as one of its objects, and to be provided with whatever is necessary for such a course. He would consult wisely for his country, and the world, who should establish foundations and scholarships for this specific object.

Another object to be kept in view in such an Institution, is the formation of a noble Theological

Library. A well-furnished and growing theological library in the city of New-York would be a boon not only to all the clergy around, but also to the whole country. We need a library to which our scholars may come, and find the works which no private means could readily procure. The necessity of this is daily increasing. It would be a source of strength to our Institution, and it would be an honor to our city. It would also be a stimulus to study; many of our ministers would prosecute their studies in special branches of theology, if they only had access to the needful books. The foundation of our present library is nobly laid in the 17,000 volumes of the Van Ess library, which were procured at a most moderate cost. This is an invaluable collection, as the basis for a library. It is unequalled by any library in the country in patristic literature, and in all the great works in ecclesiastical history. In the literature of the Reformation, and in the department of Incunabula, it is unique in this country. This collection has been increased chiefly through the donations of two or three of the wise and liberal friends of the Institution. The additions made during the last year and a half amount to about a thousand volumes. It is still deficient in the English and the modern German theological literature. In Biblical philology it is very incomplete. Of our American theology it contains only the more common books. In the theological periodicals of this country and Europe, it is meagre. There are no means of meeting its wants, excepting casual benefactions and special donations. We need the means of making an annual appropriation for this important object, as well as an immediate outlay for those departments in which it is now so painfully deficient. Books of reference for the students in their regular studies ought to be supplied in several copies. The current theological works, and the periodical theological literature, of this country and England, and to some extent of France and Germany, ought to be supplied to such an institution as they issue from the press. To the clergy of New-York and its vicinity, such a library would be an especial boon; and it would promote the theological interests of the whole country. No one can fully estimate the inherent value and real practical usefulness of such a library in such a place as New-York. A complete collection here, even of our American theological literature, would be a benefit and an honor to our land. And this is eminently the place where such a collection ought to exist.

Our Theological Seminary ought also to have ampler accommodations for students in the way of rooms, and pecuniary means for aiding them in the prosecution of their studies. More young men come to us than we can conveniently provide with suitable apartments. More would come if we could offer them as good rooms as most of our larger Seminaries have in abundance. We ought to have apartments for at least 125 students. Some of our young men, too, are obliged to teach more than is best for them in a theological course. Money for the temporary aid of those who need it, has been hitherto secured only by private and special solicitation; a solicitation which, we gratefully acknowledge, has thus far never been in vain. We ought to be in a condition to aid all who need it, according to the measure of their reasonable wants. The churches ought to do this for their young men. Students are drawn away from us by the promise of more aid, and of scholarships in other institutions. If some of our wealthier churches would establish scholarships to be filled by young men whom they might designate, or who should be placed under their care, it would be a great and wise benefaction to the cause of Christ.

All of our Professorships ought likewise to be placed on a secure basis. We would not have either the Professorships or the Seminary independent of the churches; but they surely ought to be raised above the fluctuations of commerce. The men whom we have called to fill these important posts ought not only to be creditably supported, but to be placed so as not to be exposed to the fear that a commercial reverse may deprive them of their means of support. And this ought especially to be the case in view of the fact, that the Seminary is now able to give them what is, at the best, but a mere maintenance. The present Faculty has, we believe, the full confidence of the Christian public. Coming from different parts of our land, they are still united, of one heart and mind in laboring for the Institution. The Faculty is now full; and the very increase of its numbers demands an increased expenditure. Our Christian public owe it to their own character, and to the good of Christ's church, and to the prosperity of the Seminary, that their position here be made secure and honorable.

That, in order to meet the great and growing wants of the country, an Institution of such a character is needed, no reflecting and Christian man can question. That the location of the Union Theological Seminary in New-York is admirably adapted to the highest ends of such a Seminary, needs not any evidence additional to that furnished by its very history. Of all the incidental aids to theological study and culture, such a city, from the nature of the case, offers a greater variety than can elsewhere be found. Students of different denominations, while here receiving a common training, can still worship with their own churches; students from all parts of the land meeting here, will form ties of intimacy and affection, and will thus be led to labor, during all their lives, with a higher and juster appreciation of what is best for the whole country. Upon New-York itself such an Institution cannot fail to have, in its measure, a healthful influence, fostering the love for sound learning and true science, and a wise theology, in the very heart of our great metropolis; restraining a worldly spirit, and making our wealth more subservient to the Redeemer's kingdom. Ought not this prosperous city, for its own best good, to have just such an Institution planted and fostered in the midst of it, and by its superabundant wealth? Ought it not to have a Seminary for the training of Christ's ministers, commensurate with the other noble charities, which wealth and benevolence have here founded? A city with such means and such influence, ought to do all it can to make its Christian influence felt far and wide. As our commerce goes to all the earth, let our ships bear every where, to the remote parts of our confederacy, to Oregon and to California, to India, Africa, the Mediterranean and the isles of the sea, men whom the merchants that have fitted out the ships have helped to prepare for diffusing the Gospel of Christ, that noblest work of commerce, among all the nations of the earth. What nobler object can be proposed to our Christian community, than that of building up such a Theological Seminary as our country and times need in the central city of our land, for the sake of the whole country, for the good of the earth? And when were our churches better able to engage in such a work than they now are? When can it be more easily accomplished, with less of personal sacrifice?

The need of an immediate Endowment of the Seminary.

Such has been the history, and such is the present condition of this School of the Prophets. What it ought to become, and what it may become, has also in the preceding pages been set forth. The Directors have felt that it was their duty to give to the Christian public this full exposition respecting this Institution, because they are convinced that the time has come for its ample endowment.

The Institution has been mainly upheld through the generous and frequent aid and large contributions of a comparatively small number of its friends, and by the annual collections made in many of our churches in its behalf. The Directors wish to bear their heartfelt testimony of thankfulness to those who have upheld the Seminary in its hours of trial and despondency. They acknowledge with gratitude the readiness with which our churches have responded to the appeals made to them. They do not desire or intend that the Seminary should be cut off from direct intercourse with our churches. They would not have it placed in an entirely independent position. It would not be for the best good of the Seminary that it should be so, as this might lessen the interest of the churches in its character and welfare.

But more is now required for its due support than in past years. The provision for the Professors and students is felt to be inadequate. And there is no definite prospect of an increase to the funds from the means ordinarily relied upon. The incessant stress of effort necessary in order to raise the requisite amount, is becoming unpleasant. The amount necessary to be raised from our churches from year to year, is larger than they can well give, without perhaps trespassing on other benevolent objects. The means of supporting a part of the Professorships are derived from special subscriptions which run for a limited time. And the unavoidable expenses of the Institution are increasing.

To maintain the Seminary on its present basis, about $12,000 a year are needed. This is a moderate estimate, and it does not include any provision for aid to the students. From individual subscriptions, from the legacy of Mr. Roosevelt, and from all other sources, it now receives about $5,000, leaving some $7,000 to be raised in other ways from year to year. This rather exceeds the whole amount which has been obtained when our churches have contributed most liberally, and under the most forcible representation of our wants.

The question thus presented to the friends of the Seminary is, whether it shall lead a struggling and uncertain existence, or be placed at once in a condition of safety and permanence. It never has been more prosperous than it now is; it never has had more strongly the affection and confidence of the community; it has never been in a position in which its promise of extensive usefulness was greater. It is because it has grown so much, and been so favored, that its present wants are so many and urgent. It is because the wants of our country have grown, that the wants of the Seminary have increased. It has identified itself with the great evangelical interests of the whole country; shall it not be a minister of yet greater good to all these interests? Let a wise, Christian liberality supply this fountain generously, and many streams will flow out from it to make glad the city of our God.

It has lived; it must live. Shall its life be strong and vigorous, or feeble and fluctuating? If with the encouragement which God in his providence has given to this Seminary, nothing more be done for it than has been done, are we following the guidance of his Providence? Does not that bid us strengthen the foundation of this favored school of sacred learning?

The question really resolves itself into this,—Ought there to be a Theological Seminary of the highest character in the great and growing city of New-York? If there ought to be, then it ought to be permanently endowed. The existence of such a school as this, with so much to favor it, is a point which might not be gained a second time;—it has not been the work of a day, or a year. Years, more than those of its present life, might not be enough to make another, what God in the signal dispensation of his providence has made this to be. It occupies a platform and a position more to be desired than any other might be able to secure. It can, with all confidence and sincerity, on the basis of its constitution, its history and its present character, make its appeal to a larger class of wise and moderate Christian men than could be invoked by any other. Its friends are tried, and faithful, and numerous. It has had a severe probation, and by its improvement under trials, it has won to itself a good degree in the esteem and affections of the Church; it has a united Faculty, who are adjudged adequate to their responsible work; it has a large and most valuable library, such as could not at the same cost be again procured by any institution. Surely it is most unwise to expose all these advantages to hazard; surely it is the part of Christian wisdom to build on this foundation a noble structure, if a Theological Institution of the highest character is needed in the city of New-York.

The Directors feel that they can make, with the fullest confidence, their earnest appeal to the wise and the charitable. In what way can a permanent investment of a Christian man's wealth be more judiciously made, than in building up such an Institution, for the glory of God, and for the good of Christ's church! In what better work could our churches, as such, engage, than in making for this object a special and earnest effort? And if the Seminary is to be freed from its embarrassments, and put in a safe and permanent position, now is emphatically the time.

To accomplish this object the Directors have voted that it is expedient to raise the sum of one hundred and fifty thousand dollars. This sum, in addition to what the Seminary already has, will put the Institution into a condition in which it may reasonably expect to fulfil the sacred and important objects for which it was established in the city of New-York.

www.ingramcontent.com/pod-product-compliance
Lightning Source LLC
LaVergne TN
LVHW011136110826
845150LV00008B/2377
9781418194475